Win Him Back

The Ultimate Collection to Have Him Begging For More

Jennifer Cane

Want a Free E-Book?

Signup for the Gamma Mouse Media Newsletter and pick a free e-book as a Thank You Gift.

For more details and to sign-up, visit http://www.gammamouse.com.

How to Get Your Ex-Boyfriend Back Boot Camp

Secret Tactics to Win Him Back and
Have Him Begging For More

Jennifer Cane

How to Get Your Ex-Boyfriend Back: An Overview

Do you want your ex-boyfriend back? Regardless of who is at fault in a break-up there is still a chance for two people to reconcile and get their relationship together again. Remember that nothing is impossible if you are determined and are willing to do anything to get your ex-boyfriend back.

It all started with a small misunderstanding until you or he decided that the best way to end your differences is by giving up. But what if you were wrong to decide this is the best way for both of you? And what if he also made a wrong decision in letting you go? Love is sweeter the second time around and so if you are already decided, it is time to win your ex-boyfriend back!

What you need to remember

In winning an old flame you need to remember a few things. You need to have all these important qualities so you will be able to win over any kind of situation.

- **You need a lot of patience**

  Getting your ex-back is possible but not a very easy task to accomplish. You need to have a lot of patience to be able to perform different strategies to win him back. Yes there are a lot of different techniques that you can adapt to be able to win an old flame and since you are still determining which one would best work, it may take you a few trial and error activities to be able to come up with a suitable and effective approach. At this early stage, you must remember that it will really take a lot of patience to deal with an ex especially when you have had a hard time in the past. He may still be haunted with the last time you fought or he may still refuse to talk so give him the time and the space that he is asking for. The trick is to give these unconditionally, you will find that it would be easier to approach and talk to him after he has had his space and time for himself.

- **You should be able to invest a lot of time**
  And along with patience, you must also be able to have a lot of time to spare for your ex. As mentioned, it may take time for the two of you to get settled and even you need time to clear your head and think of practical ideas. Time is also needed to plan your approach. Even if you know your ex-

boyfriend through and through, you may still need ample time to strategize your plan. But remember, the more well- planned your assault is the more likely it will succeed. And even when you are taking your time planning, you should never overlook checking up on your ex beau.

- **You must think positively**

  Do not forget to think in a positive way. Do not let negative thoughts cloud your head. If you continue to think that you can win him back then this will happen. Our brains are very efficient in accepting positive thoughts and it easily reflects on what you say or do; but if you feed your brain with negative thoughts you will only end up giving up and just doing away with your plan. If you plant positive thoughts you will never fail no matter what. You can do this for all kinds of activities and work and it will surely be a guarantee that you will never have any room for failure!

- **You must never give up**

  No matter what the scenario may be you should never give up on your quest to win him back. This will never be easy; you will find yourself questioning why you have done this in the first place. But if you really think that you two deserve each other and that no matter who is at fault, you two can still work it out then there should be no reason to give up at all.

- **You should consider all the possible options**

There are a lot of ways that you can take to win him back. Recalling and doing exactly what you did to win him during the initial days you met is one thing while there are more updated and radical ways to get him to notice you. A lot of couples around the world undergo relationship difficulties; do not treat your problems as something that is new. Take from people that have gone through the same thing; almost everyone has their share of heartaches so there are millions of options to use.

- **You need to develop a sense of self worth**
  Winning your ex-boyfriend back is taking all the possible risks to get him to notice you but please never forget that you are you. You deserve love and most of all respect. If someone that you loved most has turned

away and do not consider or give back the love that you are willing to offer with an open heart then he must not be the guy for you! Therefore, before embarking on this task, question yourself. Is this a risk worth doing or are you just angry that he does not want you anymore?

When is the best time to win him back?

The most common question that often arises in planning how to bring an old flame back is the time best suited to take action. Some people may say you should never waste time to woo him back or to "strike while the iron is hot!" But there are circumstances that you must remember that can determine the time when to win your ex back:

1. There is no time to waste when you know you are at fault. If your break up was about you being too controlling, clingy and very annoying then you have to start as soon as possible. If he has told you these reasons and you have accepted that these are mainly your faults then you should make amends right away. He may still need time to think about your relationship but it is still a good

start to tell him that you are sorry and you want to change for the better.

2. If your partner is at fault but both of you agreed to break up then you should also try to patch things up as soon as possible. The sooner you two agree to reconcile the more you two will be able to mend your differences. This situation is the ideal situation where couples may decide to reconcile as soon as possible but try to remember that you have to set some ground rules to prevent situations like this from happening in the future.

3. If you think that both of you need time to think about your differences then by all means do so. As mentioned, there is nothing impossible when it comes to love. You two can patch things up or get your man after

things are clearer and both of you have cooled down.

4. In the event that your ex has moved on and you still want him back then you need more time to plan everything out. Signs that he has moved on are he has started dating, he has started going out with his buddies or he is seen happy and contented at work or in school. You may think that it is the end for you two but actually this is the best time to plan to get to win him back. He is more focused; more mature and definitely has an open mind about relationships now that he has moved on. Subtly zeroing in on him during these times is the best plan that you can do.

5. If your ex-boyfriend has ignored you and looks like he just want to be on the other

side of the planet then you may want to rethink your strategies. Obviously he plans to ignore you for more days and weeks to come and he does not want to do anything about you. Take this as an important message that you should pay caution in winning him back. But this does not mean that you should give up on your goal of winning him back; you just need to do this slowly but surely. Plan your strategies and you will be rewarded in no time at all.

What are the signs that he is willing to come back?

Aside from determining the best time when you can come back into his life you should also watch out for the signs that he is willing to come back to your loving arms. For this particular item, you should do a little bit of investigating to determine if he is indeed thinking of coming back. Remember that men are more secretive of their feelings. Some men may have even mastered the art of hiding what they really mean and so it is your job to actually do a bit of uncovering.

1. Check him out through your mutual friends. Find out how he really feels about you and if he is ever thinking about you coming back. A sign that he is actually willing to come

back is when he has openly told his friend about it or if he has been talking about you often with his friends. Your mutual friend will sincerely tell you if you have the chance or not.

2. Find out if he is currently dating. If he is then find out about the girl that he is dating. Does the girl have any similarities to you? Does she have anything in common? You may have the same hair, complexion, body type or features and this could mean that he is still looking for someone that is similar to you. But if he is dating someone that looks very different from you then he may be trying to move on and trying to forget you somehow.

3. Check out his social networks. If you are still friends on Facebook and you still follow him

at Twitter then you may check out his stats or his tweets. Signs that he is hopelessly looking for you are stats about how lonely he feels, about pictures of you two, about places and things that you used to do. But of course do not immediately presume that these are all because of your breakup and he is willing to come back. Do a deeper investigation and check hints that he is indeed looking for you. There are no particular things that you should look for but since you know him better than anyone else then you could easily find these out by yourself.

4. Is he active in clubs or in places that he usually hangs out when he was single? If he frequents clubs and social places nowadays then he must be looking for a new company. But if he has decided to stay at home or stay

away from the social scene then you should consider that he must be avoiding people that both of you know. This is still another sign that he is also willing to reconcile and work out with you.

5. Does he wear or carry around anything that symbolizes your love? It could be a ring, a jacket or anything that you two have agreed to give to one another. This is a sure sign that he is interested in giving your relationship a try. No matter how small the token or the item may be or no matter how insignificant this may be it is still worth giving your relationship a try if he does sport or use anything that symbolizes your love.

6. Finally, do you see him in places that you two frequent? This could be a particular place in the park, eating alone in a restaurant that

you two may have been to or in places that you know are significant to you and to him. If your ex does this then surely he has thought about you and he is thinking of giving your relationship a chance.

What are the signs that he is not interested?

As much as you do not want to think that he is not interested in you anymore you still need to learn all about these so that you won't spend time wooing someone that does not really want you back in his life. Yes this could be hard but you still need to be realistic.

1. He has blocked you from his social network site. You now have no access to him via Facebook or Twitter and we all know how important or how significant this is.

2. If he has openly told his friends that he is happy to be far away from you or he has finally had the taste of freedom then there is no use wooing him back. He is basically over his head on what he has achieved.

3. If he is dating and he has openly told people that he is happy then it could be difficult to somehow woo him back. Just think about this, if he is happy then why can't you be too? Do what he is doing and maybe finally you too can achieve happiness in the arms of a new love.

4. If he has ventured into other options like studies, business or career then you may want to rethink your strategies. If you two broke up because of these reasons then he may be intent on his business or career goals. You may only be seen as a hindrance to the fulfillment of his goals.

5. Finally, a sign that he is not really into you anymore if he has turned to the opposite sex. Try to keep an open mind that this situation really does exist! Some men do not

actually find out that they are homosexual until they have had a straight relationship. Apparently they have found out that they are not satisfied with a female partner and they have opened up to the possibility of loving someone of the same gender.

How to win your ex-boyfriend back

Every strategy in winning an ex flame back takes time and careful planning. You simply just cannot charge into the battlefield without figuring out your offense. Take your time. It may not happen today or tomorrow but when it does, he may never be able to resist you because you have planned long and hard for your assault!

The self-realization stages

Every planning starts with a realization. Do you really want your boyfriend back or you are just curious if you can still catch his attention and beg for you to take him back? No matter what the reason may be, it is healthy to sort out your feelings and settle really what the deeper reason for your actions.

The best way to come up with a good self-realization output is to write down your feelings and then make a reflection. For instance, you broke up after he has become very controlling and very physical on you; would you still want to come back to this kind of unhealthy relationship? If you two broke up because of a third party then would you be willing to take him back after he has cheated on you? Weigh all these and if your love and your trust still weighs more than his flaws and all your differences then you may proceed with planning your strategy.

The planning stages

Just like any kind of planning for anything in your life you need to concentrate, sit down and pour all your best efforts in coming up with a feasible and efficient idea. Here are some great ideas on how to proceed with planning:

1. Clear your mind and remove all the anger and the negative emotions and concentrate on the positive things about your relationship. Remove all the fighting and the bickering and take inspiration on the times when you were able to work together or had a good time together. You will find that it is easier to find a feasible solution when you focus on the positive instead of all the negative feelings.

2. Get a good rest. If you are tired you will never be able to find a suitable solution for your problems. If you must take a short vacation to plan then you should indulge in one. You may also do some relaxation activities like go to a spa, do yoga or meditation so you will become relaxed and ready for any suggestions.

3. Take some hints from people you trust. Turn off that television! There is no use patterning your love life from movies and television series. Yes you can make these as your inspiration but you must take advice from real people that have gone through real breakup situations. Ask your parents, friends, family members or colleagues at work. By taking advice from people that you personally know you will be able to use their advice in a practical manner. Other people

that you may ask for help are psychiatrists, your pastor, your manager or anyone significant in your work or family.

4. Be realistic. Plan using pen and paper. Do not immediately plan and do the plan right away but instead test your theories out. For instance you are planning on relieving the day you have met by dressing or basically looking just like the person that he fell in love with when he first met you. Test this out first by suggesting small hints. Wear something that he is familiar with or play a song that you two once enjoyed listening together. If you find some change and that it looks like you have caught his attention then considers this as a part of your plan.

5. Plan a lot of different plans. If you have a lot of time in your hands then you could create

different plans: A, B, C and so on. Do not give up if you think that you are fighting for what is right! Create a file on your computer about your plans, write them down or illustrate them; you are doing these to basically motivate you.

6. Plan with someone you trust. Now do not be afraid to plan and strategize with someone you trust. Remember two heads are better than one after all! With a planning partner you could have someone that can immediately evaluate your plans and to help you come up with creative ones. If possible, the person that could help you is a mutual friend or someone that both of you trusts. Your partner should also be a person that can help you with evaluating if the plan that you have just done had a positive or negative effect. And with all these potential

things that your partner has to do, it is no wonder that this person has to be someone that you two can trust.

The ways to win him back

Finally, here are some winning strategies to woo your ex-boyfriend back. All these strategies have been tried and tested by couples around the world. These strategies are classified according to their degree of skill and patience.

Relieving the day you met

Possibly one way to win him is to be just like the person that he fell in love with years or months ago. And since you may not be able to talk to him yet you may do this by wearing your hair the same style you had, the same dress you wore or the same accessories that you had on. Anyone that has felt how to be in love will understand the feeling of seeing his old flame looking just like what you remembered her. And of course you will get an instant reaction too!

A few tips to pull this off:

1. Do not immediately affirm that you are really doing this on purpose if he asks you. Simply shrug off his attempts to ask you if you are seducing or trying to catch his attention. Remember that now that you have his attention, you now have him in the palm of your hands.

2. Act natural; do not immediately react to teasing and pressure from your peers. Simply smile and look at him just like what you used to before. You know that you got him in your spell when he starts to notice and makes an effort to converse with you.

3. Keep your distance but at the same time stay in his complete view.

4. If he still does not notice or seems to pretend that he does not care then this is time you approach him and ask some trivial questions first, the rest will certainly follow to signal that he is still interested in you.

Flaunt what he has lost

You will be reinventing yourself by looking healthier, smarter and fitter. All these are a clear message to him he has lost someone as beautiful, smart and alluring! This strategy is basically one of the most efficient and the most practical because men are very critical in most things. Women may simply take intuition as one of the best ways to decide on tings while men may weigh things before they make a decision. You can show him what he has lost with the following strategies.

1. Get a new look that he likes. If he liked you with long hair then visit the salon to have yours straightened or wear hair extensions. Wear makeup to highlight your great features and to cover some of your flaws.

2. Go on a diet or go to the gym and try to lose weight. He will certainly drool with passion when he sees the person that he has wronged. At the gym, try to work your problem areas goodbye like a flabby midsection, upper arms and behind. Talk to a gym instructor on how you can lose weight and remove these unsightly areas. Remember, men are very keen on any physical changes and they will immediately notice that there are some changes from your figure as soon as they meet you.

3. Change your wardrobe. There are women that do not have anything wrong with their figure but are just unaware of the best way to flaunt it. You may take lessons from designers, online personal stylists and wardrobe stylists. This goes for women that dress inappropriately like not dressing your age or dresses from styles stuck in a forgotten era. It won't hurt to make a wardrobe overhaul! By doing so you are embracing change and this is good. Your ex will certainly notice this and appreciate the changes that you may have done with your looks and wardrobe.

Important tips to pull this technique off

1. A physical change is a great step to winning your man since you are sacrificing a lot of

time and effort in making sure you look good and you feel good about yourself. And you are not just doing this for your ex-boyfriend but you are also doing this for your own sake.

2. Don't immediately approach your man and say "notice something new?" Give him an in your face ignorant look that could mean you are unaware of the changes that has happened. For once, offer an air of mystery even when people around you are checking out the changes that they see. Simply shrug all these things off and tell them that you have changed and that's it.

3. Let him drool over you. Watch him watch you from afar and if you can, have someone check his reaction out. Ask a friend to take expert evaluations on how you made an

impact on his senses. If this strategy worked well then it is time to go for the kill.

Ask him out

But this is not a romantic date. This is a sort of "for all-time's sake" date. Let him decide on the place where he would like to go. You need to let him pick the venue since it is through his decisions will you be able to sense if you still have that effect on him. If he picked a place where you two have gone before then this is a good sign but if he takes you someplace else then this may still be okay. Do not jump the heavens when he does agree to go out but act cool and unaffected. Be sure to keep these tips in mind:

1. Set this date as soon as possible. You must strike when the iron is hot.

2. And even when you are raring to hug or kiss him, restrain yourself! Keep a few inches apart from him. Converse with eye contact and do not lose interest in what he is saying.

3. Remember the things that he may not like about you before (being over protective, being controlling and dominant), remove this negative attitude as much as possible and make sure that you remind yourself that this is not yet the goal that you wish to attain!

4. If you two are off to a restaurant or a bar to drink, order something nonalcoholic so you will avoid getting intoxicated. Remember that you plan on making this date a memorable one and you do not want to have a hangover and forget what have just happened. Talk about life and please refrain

on talking about your past or your break up. Just talk about what has happened today and how he has been. If he asks you if you miss him then sincerely say that you do and then change the subject. This is a way to keep him hanging on to your every word.

5. If he complements you on your new looks then be gracious about it. You do not have to ask him if he like it or not since it is pretty obvious that he is into you. Simply accept his kind remarks and focus on your goal and that it so eventually win him over.

6. When he hints on a second date then you have succeeded in your plan! You have made him interested and now he will certainly be very eager to see you again! If you two meet at work or at school, take this time to simply smile and wave to him and

that is it. Maintain your composure even when you are dying to talk to him. Make him beg for your attention. He may try to call you, send you emails or go out of his way to ask you how you have been and these are definitely good signs that your plan is working out.

On your second date, stay as vibrant and as entertaining as you can be but still keep a small distance. If he tries to do some moves (ask you personal questions, try to be closer or try to intimidate you) dismiss it. He will certainly make a few remarks on how he would like to do something or what he intends to do with you and now this is the best time to tell him that you would like him to ask for you (of course in a funny or charming way!) Men love challenges and they will see it that this is one and immediately ask what you want from him.

THIS IS THE TIME YOU ARE LOOKING FOR! Lay down your cards and wait for his reaction.

Other ways to lure him towards you

1. Men love food and most will find food irresistible especially served with love. If you used to cook for your man or he adores your cooking, then you can say that you want him back by sending him a cake or a delicious pastry that you know he likes. He will surely be begging to come back for more.

2. Find things that both of you love to do. This could be any activity like sports, camping, motor racing, cars, chess, and computer games, gardening or reading books. By finding a common ground between the both of you, you will be able to expertly lure him to your company and get him to where you want him to be.

- Invite him in a car show or to an upcoming racing event that you two have been planning to go.

- Ask him if he could accompany you to a book signing even as friends. Rekindle your love for each other as you read books that you two love.

- Talk about things that you know he is interested him and ask for his expert opinion. For instance, you may ask for his expert gardening techniques to help you with your new herb garden or ask him about a computer game cheat that you have been working on.

- Invite him to a camping event as friends and find activities that you two can share together like tent pitching, fishing, camp activities and so many more.

3. Do the damsel in distress strategy. If your ex loves to help people in need then pretend that you desperately need his help. But be sure to make this believable that he won't suspect a thing. This may be anything as simple as car trouble in the middle of nowhere or as complicated as being locked in an elevator! You can expertly pull this off as you embrace him lovingly and as terrified as you can look and sound like. He will find this an ego boosting situation and will certainly never leave your side to protect you in the future (if your plan works perfectly!).

Winning your ex-boyfriend and keeping him forever is the key to these strategies but most of all you should change the negative attitude that may have led to your breakup in the first place. If for some great reason you two have decided to forgive and forget and patch things up then strive to make your relationship healthy. Have open communication and settle differences as soon as possible to avoid potential problems in the future.

Putting it all together...

Now that I have given you all the tools you will need to win back your ex-boyfriend, it is time to take action and implement the advice in this guide. No guy will come back to you if you only wish and hope, you need to make him beg to come back.

I hope you have found this guide helpful and informative. May you truly get the relationship you desire.

Good luck!

Text Dating

A Girl's Guide to Texting and
Winning over Your Dream Guy

Jennifer Cane

How to Get Him to Notice You

Texting is a great way for women to try to get guys to want to date them. Love can take a great deal of hard work. In today's day and age, technology has helped with matters of the heart. Here are some tips on how to get a guy to notice your texts.

Be Flirtatious with Your Texts

Men love being chased. Flirting is a great way to get a guy's attention. Use language like, you are so cute, I saw you today and my heart stopped. Clichés can be a great way to make him notice the text. Guys love attention and they want girls to dote on them. Text him every few hours. This will make it much harder for him to ignore your texts.

Text Him When You Know He Is Not Busy

People often have hectic schedules. Try timing your texts with holes in his schedules so that he is more likely to see the texts and be able to respond to them quickly. If the guy is in high school or college then try to avoid texting him during the school day as he might not hear the phone if it makes a sound during class or is turned off.

Try Being Outrageous

Guys like to laugh. Outrageously funny texts are memorable and will make an impact on him. A guy doesn't want to just read a text that says hello or how are you. They want a funny joke that will make them smile and laugh. If you can catch his eye with a great one liner then he is sure to text you back more frequently.

Consider Using a Conversation Starter

Texts that can spark conversations often will catch the eye of a guy. Think about topics that he is interested such as sports or cars. Text him some information about a breaking news story and ask for his opinion on the matter. This move can be a great one because guys often feel like girls do not care about their opinions. This can impress him and make him feel like his point of view is actually valuable.

Do Not Respond Right Away

Playing hard to get can actually be a good thing. If he does text you back, then don't respond immediately. Make him wait 15 to 30 minutes. This can actually make him more eager for your response. It also shows that you might not be waiting by the phone every time he texts you. Men actually become more excited by this.

Consider Texting Him Lyrics to Songs That He Likes

Guys appreciate it when a girl makes a huge effort to try to reach out to them. Do some research and ask people that know him if they know songs that he like. Go online and try to find the lyrics. Then, you can begin to copy them into a text and send them to him. Try to also include a sweet message such as your smile made me think of this song. He will text you back if he finds the gesture romantic. With these tips, you should begin a relationship in no time.

How to Drive Him Crazy

A long time ago, when people liked each other, they would write sappy love letters with the intention of expressing how much they desired each other and how they could not wait to meet again. Times have changed and nowadays, love letters have been replaced with endless text messages, quick phone calls and messaging apps that make it so much easier to keep in touch, without getting too personal.

Texting a guy you like is a delicate balancing act. On the one hand, you want to keep in touch and glimpse a few things about him; on the other, you do not want to come off desperate and annoying. So, how does a girl, infatuated, ensure the object of her affection keeps desiring her long after the numbers have been exchanged?

Here's how to raise desire when you text a guy:

First things first. Don't text first.

Yes, you met this ridiculously cute and charming guy at the bar last night and you exchanged numbers but guess what, that's not a cue to blow up his phone with numerous, meaningless and intrusive text messages. The trick is to keep calm and wait for him to text first. The surest way to turn off a guy who asked for your number is to be the first one to text him, as this looks desperate and needy.

Don't text immediately.

When the cute charmer texts you, don't reply within nanoseconds. It will seem as if you've been desperately sitting by your phone waiting for him to text. And while this may be so, there's no need to make it obvious. A girl who has a life is actually very desirable. Wait for five or so minutes before replying and when you do...

Make it short and sweet.

If you want a guy to desire you, send him short and sweet texts. Don't write down your entire life history for him. He does not need to know that. Share tidbits about yourself and you'll keep him guessing. A mysterious woman is intriguing and intrigue always keeps the guy coming for more.

Make him laugh.

Boring text messages are the surest way to get ignored by your new love interest. Do not be afraid to show your funny side. That being said, don't try too hard.

Flirt a little.

Depending on how long you've been texting, a little teasing here and there is always welcome. Of course, you don't want to start flirting immediately as this may cloud his impression of you.

Be interesting.

Steer the conversation towards topics of interest. Do not be afraid to show your intelligence through your texts. Get him thinking and he'll have you on his mind for a long time. As with the humor, do not overdo it; it's not a competition.

Know when to end the conversation.

A good rule all women need to learn when texting is when and how to end the conversation. If you get to that point where you're struggling to find things to talk about, end the conversation right away. Do not drag it on forever. Also, if you can ensure he never gets to end the conversation you'll keep him eagerly waiting for a next time.

When ending the conversation, don't just say "Bye" or "See ya!"; instead, leave the conversation open so that next time you start chatting you can pick it up from there. For instance you could mention you are going out to a concert with your friends or something similar. The next time you chat, he'll have the opportunity to ask how the concert was and so on.

And that's how to keep a guy tuned to your channel...well, as far as texting goes!

What You Should Never Do When Texting a Guy

So, you have noticed a guy and you like him. You are probably wondering what you should text him. Sometimes the heart gets too overwhelmed and you cannot stop yourself from sending a message. However, before you pick your phone to compose a text you should stop and think. You need to learn the tips not only on what to text a guy, but also what you should never do when texting a guy you like.

Do not drink before texting:

You may feel that you need the extra 'alcohol courage' to write to the guy about what you feel about him.

This is a very wrong move, because your thought process will be compromised. Trust me, you do not want to wake up nursing a hangover, only to gasp in shame at the text you sent the guy you like. Stay sober before composing anything.

Declare love:

Granted, what you may be feeling in you might be love. You could be falling asleep to the thoughts of the guy you like, and waking up to the same. However, do not put that in writing. You will come off as needy, desperate and weird. Men love doing the chase, so do not make yourself too available. It will scare him away.

Send many texts:

If you had sent previous texts that were not responded to, do not send others. There could be reasons why he is not replying to your texts, one of them being that he does not want you to text him. Whatever his reason for not texting back is, respect it. Do not keep pressuring him by piling more messages on him hoping that he will reply. One text is enough. Until he responds to it, refrain from sending many others.

Sending your nudes:

There is a new wave that is sweeping people: sending nude photos. Technology now allows you to snap a photo of your privates, and send it immediately via texts. It is never a good idea. For one, you will definitely look cheap, and second you do not want to imagine how far your photos can spend. There are never any exceptions when it comes to texting your nudes, especially to a guy you like. Keep your texts general and light.

Tell religious, sexual or discriminatory jokes:

During the first stages of texting, avoid jokes that may be found offensive. In fact, unless you think you are really funny, do not struggle with cracking jokes because they may backfire. Lean more towards knowing the guy and making him know you.

Let him do all the work for you:

If you are texting each other, do not let the guy do all the work. It is boring to keep responding to all texts with emojis, or one word sentences. You should try keeping up with the conversation. Ask questions, share your opinions, and get with the flow. You may think it is easy for guys to come up with text messages to send, but sometimes it takes time. So show some appreciation by texting back with something interesting that will get a response from him.

The Best Way to Ask a Guy Out

It is very difficult for a lady to ask a guy out on a one on one conversation. This is due to the fact that the lady might seem so desperate for a date. In addition, there is always the fear of rejection which can be very embarrassing. The only solution to such a problem is the use of text messaging. As a matter of fact, text messaging is known to be the most common way of chatting. This creates a very good platform for individuals to pour out their affection and love for one another.

Come up with a convincing idea to go out

When asking a guy out, you must have a convincing reason and idea as a lady. This is because not all guys are welcome to treats by ladies hence a convincing idea can serve the purpose best. In this case, do not formulate a lie but instead for instance, you can inquire on the individual's free time so as to ascertain the best time for the out.

Spearhead the conversation

Once you have the perfect idea to convince your guy out, take action and begin a conversation. To not go straight to the idea of the date but instead start with a discussion that will lead to that topic. For instance, you can discuss your favorite drinks and as a result, you may end up convincing your guy to try it out with you.

Maintain intimacy during the conversation

For you to completely and properly convince a guy to go out with you, he must feel your love. Introduce some romantic and sensual conversations that will melt down his heart. Do not flirt. That is the worst mistake you can make in such a moment. Flirting definitely informs the guy that you are testing him and not really asking him out. Avoid boring conversations that could send your guy to sleep but instead engage in a humorous discussion that will send him into gales of laughter.

Ask the guy out

Asking the guy out can be the very challenging part of the entire discussion since you might not be aware of where or how to begin. However, there is nothing for you to panic about. When asking the guy out, make it appear like something usual. Tell him that you have a surprise for him. Try as much as possible not to disclose it to him. You can tell him that you want to show him a friend of yours who has just come to town. Through this, he will barely have an idea of what awaits him.

How to know that your invite was accepted

Once you have asked your guy out, you are not completely certain that he is in for it. However, there are some reactions that can tell it all. Statements such as "I look forward to your surprise" or "I am in" can be indicators that your guy is willing to go out with you. He might also ask questions about the meeting place and time. This means that he has fallen for you invitation and now it is up to you

to make it a reality.

Cute Texts That Will Win Him Over

Hey girls, text messaging is the new way to turn on a man! Shortly, I will be outlining tips for you to use in winning him completely and have him for yourself. This is not magic, it is just but simple advise from a woman who has studied the behavior of men and willing to help you explore some of the tricks each woman should use when "shopping" for a date with a man, be it Virgin Atlantic top managers or even the who is who in Facebook and Twitter.

Here are 10 Tips to Get a Man Wanting More through Texts:

1. Promise to meet him at some day

Ladies, men are like babies, they will always listen to what a woman says no matter what happens. When a man asks you to meet him, do not hesitate to promise him that you will meet him some day. Do not commit to a date in your first text; simply make a promise to make him eager.

2. Be the first!

Initiate the conversation with him then hold back. When you do that, it will trigger his interest. Do not give an answer straight away, keep him waiting, soon you will see him bothering you with a chain of messages. The idea is to turn on his mind, then wait for his response. As they say every action, there is always a reaction. Be the action yourself.

3. Act Busy

Use delaying tactics when responding to a man's text message. Fake business, tell him you are doing your accounting for the day but promise to get back later on. Once you do that, he will just think you are not that cheap girl in the street. After some few hours, get back to him with a well-crafted message that you are thankful for his previous message.

4. Give him a plan

Every man needs a focused woman. Tell him of your career and ask him what he is doing on his part. Unleash a grand plan for your future, that way you will win him to his side. No man ever wants a woman who will be a "parasite" in his life or just a mere Gold Digger.

5. Send a Multi Media Text of yourself

Drop him a text of your best photo and make sure it does not portray any nudity that could piss him off. I guarantee you that he will keep staring at your photo until that moment you decide to meet him.

6. Keep him waiting and apologize later

When he sends you a text, make it a choice or design to ignore it. He will get irritable but will not want to show or vent his anger on you. Later on, apologize for having to wait for your reply.

7. Fake it until you make it

Never expose your true personality that early. If you think you are hot tempered or nagging, please hold your horses; you do not want to lose your dream man.

8. Do not get into details

When replying to his texts, never ever elaborate anything. Let him dissect your information as it is. This will make him ask you little more questions to keep the conversation going.

9. Cram his calendar

Drop him messages at his most convenient time. Do not intrude into his work time, you should not seem like you are begging for some attention from him. Once you learn his calendar, you can even ask him how his day was and put yourself in his shoes.

10. Flirting is key

Tell him you love his new shirt. You should get reply text within a few seconds. After all which man does not desire praise and recognition.

These tips will go a long way in helping all women in securing a date with the man of their choice. Remember to start and keep him waiting, arouse his eagerness and most importantly fake it until you make it.

Text Dating – You've Got to Make It Happen

I hope that you have found this girl's guide to text dating helpful and informative. My hope is that this has given you a foundation in which to build upon.

Good luck in all your future relationship endeavors.

Free Bonus Book

Thank you so much for your purchase. As an additional bonus we are including another great book, Ketogenic Diet by Nicole Harrington for you.

I hope you enjoy!

Ketogenic Diet

The Effective and Safe Way to Lose
Weight and Regain Your Life

Nicole Harrington

The Amazing Ketogenic Diet

The idea of ketogenic dieting is not peculiar. As a matter of facts, ketogenic diet has been there in many forms and in many variations. It has got many similarities to the Atkins diet. By the end of this article, you will be able to find what exactly ketogenic diet is, how and reasons why it works. Otherwise, it is good to note that, ketogenic exists in three different types: the Targeted ketogenic diet, cyclical ketogenic diet and the Standard Ketogenic diet. They are almost the same but differ according to limits and timing of carbohydrates consumption.

So, what is the Ketogenic diet?

In simple terms, ketogenic diet can be defined as any diet that forces the body in a process known as the Ketosis, whereby extra fats are burned as an alternative of carbohydrates which is used as energy. The right ketogenic diet requires the dieter to consume high amount of fat, sufficient amounts of protein and very small amounts of carbohydrates. It is also good to note that, bodies are of the character that, they turn extra carbohydrate in glucose which is sent to all over the body in energy form. When you enter ketosis by sufficiently restricting your carbohydrate consumption, your livers begin breaking down fat cells into fatty acids and ketones, which is supposed to be used as the energy.

How does ketogenic diet work?

Just like any other diet that you know of, ketogenic diet works by reducing the amount of calories you consume, in turn creates a caloric shortfall where the body burns more energy than it takes. That is the basic science of weight loss, and even though the argument is subjected to further debating, few shall be of the opinion that, all successful diets depends on caloric limitation, in one way or another. The following are some of the advantages of ketogenic diet:

It helps in controlling blood sugar and minimizing insulin spikes

When you consume carbohydrates, your blood sugar level would increase tremendously; this will also cause the fast insulin reaction from the pancreatic gland. This insulin is useful in dispersing excess blood glucose, which makes you to feel hungry almost immediately. And if you eat a low carbohydrate diet, you succeed in keeping your blood sugar levels low and hence the carb that induces hunger spikes are avoided. Reducing hormone level is the top priority for any diet so does ketogenic diet. Insulin should be reduced because it is the hormone that induces the body to store fat.

Ketogenic diet enables the body consume food that is satiating and filling

Those who have eaten ketogenic diet do find it extremely easy to limit calories. If you are using this diet in the right way, you will be able to consume quite a good amount of calories daily ranging from fats to protein which is both satiating and scrumptious. Those are in ketogenic diet would find it hard to consume enough food every day.

Finally, ketogenic diets have become more popular for many reasons. A part from helping weight loss, it is being considered as the possible treatment or prevention of epilepsy and researches have also shown that it can also be used in neurological conditions. Having known what the ketogenic diet is, you can try it if you have used it and you will be dumbfounded. Ketogenic diet is highly recommended.

Is the Ketogenic Diet Right For Me?

Benefits of the Ketogenic Diet

The benefits if ketogenic diet are numerous and happy ones. Some of the benefits one may expect after switching to ketogenic diet include:

It is always important to get a full blood lipid panel before starting on this diet so one can compare their blood work after starting on the diet.

Lower blood pressure

Ketogenic diets are effective in lowering the blood pressure. Though, if one is taking blood pressure medication, they should be aware that they begin to feel dizzy or tipsy from too much medication while on this diet. It is advisable for people suffering from blood pressure related diseases to seek a doctor's advice before starting on this diet

A drop in cholesterol

Cholesterol is usually made out of excess glucose. This diet requires one to consume less sugar foods which simply mean a reduction in the excess glucose. The body cholesterol will drop as the body has less glucose to make cholesterol

A drop in triglycerides

Consumption of carbohydrates is closely attached to triglycerides levels. This is the most well-known ketogenic diet advantage. The less the carbohydrates consumed, the lower the triglycerides readings will go. The triglycerides: HDL ratio is the best indicator of heart attack risk and is one of the blood test one should pay attention to. The best ration is 1:1 which suggests that one is healthy.

Weight loss

Adhering to a ketogenic diet plan might be extremely effective for normalizing your weight. However, if one has high fasting insulin, he/she may be required to add a high intensity program (an exercise one). Training has a high effect on increasing the sensitivity of the body to insulin.

What to watch out for on the diet

Disadvantages of ketogenic diet plan are mostly due to its side effects. Some of the side effects are extreme.

Frequent urination

This is because the body is burning the extra glycogen stored in the liver and muscles. This process releases a lot of water which is given out as urine.

Exhaustion and Dizziness

As the body gets rid of excess water, the body will lose minerals like salt, magnesium and potassium. Lower levels of these minerals will lead to a person becoming tired or very dizzy. This is amongst the well-known side effect of any low carbohydrate diet and the best way to overcome this is to keep replacing the minerals. This can be done by eating leafy vegetables (potassium), magnesium citrate (magnesium) or any other foods that contain the minerals.

Constipation

This is also common with most low carb diets and is usually caused by salt loss, dehydration and magnesium deficiency. This can be controlled by drinking more water and replacing the above minerals

Muscle cramps

This is due to loss of minerals particularly magnesium. It is therefore recommended that a person takes 3 slow discharge magnesium tablets like Slow-Mag for 20 days, and then keep on taking one tablet after wards

Diarrhea

There is need to limit the amount of fat you consume while on the ketogenic diet plan as this results to consuming more proteins. High proteins, low fat and low carbohydrate levels causes signs of "rabbit starvation". It is therefore advisable to replace the carbohydrates with fats, for example, butter or coconut oil and not proteins.

The Building Blocks of the Ketogenic Diet

A ketogenic diet is composed of a variety of foods that have their own health benefits and purposes. Many individuals with specific medical conditions or health goals prefer this diet because of its nutrition as well as having a variety of common foods that don't have to be eliminated from their original diet.

Proteins

A major part of the ketogenic diet is meat because it's the major source of protein. Beef, chicken and fish are important part of the diet because they supply the needed nutrients for the body. For individuals who aren't big fans of meat, tofu is also a great source of protein (and very common among vegans because it doesn't have any animal products). Cheese is also often eaten for its protein benefits but it also has some health set-backs like the high amount of calories and fat, so it's limited in the diet. Many other dairy products that are high in fat are eaten. Whole eggs are some of the most well-known contributors of protein in just about any diet. If possibly, try to purchase range-free eggs and you can also add them to other dishes.

Carbohydrates

Fruits and vegetables are the healthy and most common source of carbohydrates in this diet. Salads with leafy greens, green beans and carrots are the preferable vegetables. Peaches, berries and applause are the most common fruit that can be eaten alone by itself or added to other foods as a topping. Both vegetables and fruits also have many necessary vitamins and can be prepared many different ways, or even eaten uncooked. There are also many pasta substitutes that replace original whole grains, contributing with their nutrients. Spices like sea salt and black pepper also provide this important nutrient.

Fats

Fats compose the majority of the daily caloric intake in the ketogenic diet. They are very important to the body but some fats are very unhealthy and even dangerous to consume, so be cautious. To balance out the nutrients, foods like tuna and shellfish are commonly eaten. Some individuals also like to consume different types of oils (coconut, vegetable, olive, etc.) and add butters to their meat and other foods. Some of the healthiest sources of healthy fat are avocados, but you are also free to try almonds and other delicious nuts.

Beverages

In this diet, dehydration is fairly common so it's important to keep the body functioning properly with liquids. Of course the most basic liquid consumed by practically everyone is water, drink plenty of it! Sometimes coffee will provide a good energy boost as well. All types of teas are welcome, fruit, herbal or others. The more liquids in the body, the better. Liquid sweeteners like Stevia and Erythritol can be added to the tea or coffee for a sweet boost and extra flavor.

The Ketogenic diet is very unique and practically the opposite of the vegan diet. Make sure you consume all the nutrients you need for the day and this diet can have many positive effects on your health and body.

What to Avoid on the Ketogenic Diet

Many methods of losing some weight and maintaining a healthy and fitting body are evolving over time. Selecting the right diet, taking weight loss pills, doing exercises, and surgical methods are a few examples to get rid of excess fat cells from the body. While some of these methods may work perfectly, others may not only have insignificant effects, but also come with side-effects. One of the most effective methods is to practice the Ketogenic diet plan. It is a low-carbohydrate, adequate protein, and high-fat diet geared at burning excess fats. With this low carbohydrate diet plan, the aim is not to restrict intake of calories, but to reduce the amount of sugar and carbohydrate consumption.

What foods to avoid

On this plan, one should avoid food high in sugars, carbohydrates, and unhealthy fats. These diets are not only toxic to the human body, but they also supply the body with excess glucose that is then stored as fat cells. Since they raise blood sugars and insulin levels in the body, it becomes hard for the human body to lose more fats. In addition, human body digests and absorbs food high in carbohydrates faster than in fats or proteins. These processes not only lower metabolism, but also make the person hungry faster than normal, hence increasing the chances of the person consuming more calories that may lead to weight gain. The following is what to avoid on the ketogenic diet at all cost.

Junk or fast foods

These foods do not only contain high amounts of saturated salts and cholesterol, but they also lack essential nutrients the body require to remain healthy. Hot dogs, French fries, and soft sodas are a few examples of these foods. In addition, they contain chemicals and other substances that lower the body metabolism. With low metabolism, the body is unable to burn the food that a person takes, but instead stores it as fats. This effect does not only lead to weight gain, but to other complications such as hardening and narrowing of arteries hence resulting in high blood pressure or diabetes.

Some fruits and vegetables

One should avoid fruits that contain high amounts of carbohydrates. A few examples of such fruits are olive, watermelon, apricots, cranberry, bananas, and strawberry. It is also advisable to avoid the juices that come from these fruits since they do not only contain high carbohydrates, but they also have other artificial addictions harmful to the body. In addition, one should avoid vegetables that grow beneath the earth like onions, carrots, and potatoes for their high carbohydrate contents.

Alcohol

Even though the alcohol may contain no carbohydrates, research show that it slows down the fat burning processes in the body. It is better for one to take free sugar drinks like scotch and vodka, instead of alcohol.

Grain products

It is best for the person on the ketogenic diet to avoid grains and their products that contain high carbohydrates. Examples include white bread, white pasta, what rice, cakes, and pastries. In addition, avoid packaged or processed foods since they contain preservatives and other additions harmful to the body.

Frequently Asked Questions about the Ketogenic Diet

The ketogenic diet was founded in 1920 by Lyle McDonald. It is a very popular diet and is followed worldwide. The ketogenic diet is effective in preventing crises of many kinds as lesser carbohydrates from starches composed of glucose are consumed by the body. After this diet, it is necessary to avoid foods containing carbohydrates like bread, sugar, cereals, pasta and potatoes.

The ketogenic diet has been the staple food for people living in the countryside and also with the Eskimos and many tribes and who basically eat pure protein. During ketosis brain cells are able to get energy from fat instead of glucose. In fact the brain cannot consume fatty acids but uses only ketones or ketone bodies generated during fat metabolism.

Not only is the nervous system not damaged but it has been demonstrated by studies that brain ketosis acts as protective measure against toxic substances like free radicals and prevents hypoxia. Ketogenic diets are recommended by doctors to treat childhood epilepsy or diseases like Alzheimer.

The Ketogenic Diet

The ketogenic diet has been proven to work effectively for a third of patients who become tried and listless after very little effort. Controlled trials have established that a ketogenic diet is found to be effective in the treatment of severe epilepsy in children and adults. Although this diet is very popular among bodybuilders, it does not recommend consumption of foods which are rich in vitamins and minerals, such as broccoli, carrots, sweet potatoes, apples, grapes, raisins, figs, etc.

A Sample Meal Plan for the Ketogenic Diet

Breakfast - Two eggs, two slices of bacon and a boiled tomato.

Lunch - Hamburger meat wrapped in lettuce.

Dinner - Green beans, fried mushrooms and linseed oil with a salmon fillet red peppers.

Snacks - Unlimited yogurt and whole milk, cheese, strawberries with cream, peanut butter.

Frequently asked questions about the effects of a ketogenic diet:

Does the ketogenic diet have negative consequences in the liver or kidneys?

The ketogenic diet or diets based on eating fewer carbohydrates do not have any liver or renal type problems because it is a physiological process for which we are adapted by our own evolution and in fact people who have this type of problems are advised to take a ketogenic diet in many cases.

Is the ketogenic diet carcinogenic?

It has also been shown that the ketogenic diet helps shrink tumours and reduce the percentage of body fat and weight in the most obese people, yes factor that facilitates the development of cancer.

Does a ketogenic diet produce oxidation of cells?

Ketogenic diets increase the antioxidant capacity of the body is increased because oxygenate ketones mitochondria through activation of glutathione peroxidase producing an increase in the synthesis of mitochondrial glutathione. Antioxidants prevent the formation of free radicals thereby preventing oxidation and preventing cell death.

Is a ketogenic diet detrimental to participation in sports?

Many athletes use the ketogenic diet in combination with physical training and use key ketogenic supplements with their diet plan. This obviously needs some knowledge and experience and it is recommended to take the advice from a specialist in ketogenic diets and exercise.

The Ketogenic Diet and Diabetes

Before the invention of insulin in 1920s, the treatment of diabetes relied on dietary control. Diabetics were recommended to modify their diet to control the level of glucose in the blood circulation.

A ketogenic diet is comprised of low-carbohydrate amount. The diet has high fat content that supplements the carbohydrates. Fat is broken down and replaces glucose as a source of energy. The ketogenic diet has only enough protein for body growth.

Less carbohydrate in the diet lead the body to take measures and source for alternative source of energy. The liver releases stored glycogen that is converted to glucose. When the stores are exhausted the body turns to fatty acids replacing glucose.

Proteins are converted to glucose and the body is able to maintain normal blood sugar levels without ingesting carbohydrates. The body can effectively rely on fats for energy functions. Ingestion of insulin is accompanied by health problems. High insulin levels result to weight gain and fat storage sometimes accompanied by heart problems.

A ketogenic diet for diabetics is meant to reduce medical treatment of diabetes. Low carbohydrate in the diet prevents short term effects of diabetes and delays long term complications. The treatment of diabetes requires that medical attention is given continuously. Patients who manage their diet have a better chance of avoiding complications. Low carbohydrate diet leads to the benefit of weight loss and reduces the risk for cholesterol.

When carbohydrates are ingested, the body breaks them into glucose and other simple sugars. The glucose is taken into the blood system. A diet with more carbohydrates leads to toxic levels of blood sugar and the body responds by releasing insulin with the aim of converting glucose to glycogen for storage.

Diabetes occurs when the body does not produce enough insulin to cope with blood sugar after meals. The disease has become common of lately and the solution is to cut on carbohydrates and there will be no need for insulin.

Ketogenic diet is a complement of treatment for diabetes. This requirement of insulin can go as low as 50% easing the treatment procedure. The liver is able to produce glucose from proteins and the brain can rely on this. Some part of the brain only burns glucose for energy. Other parts of the body can rely entirely of fats for energy. With normal fat stores a person can go for days without eating.

Ketogenic diet appears to the body as starvation. The response is reduced insulin production. Oxidation of fatty acids increases to produce energy for body functions.

This method of diabetes treatment is advantageous because it deals with the root source. The aim is to reduce carbohydrates consumption, which is safer than injecting insulin to counteract high glucose level. The diet can be used where insulin is applied and faster results will be observed.

Fighting diabetes can be challenging because of the change in diet and lifestyle. The patients are sometimes mislead and filled with wrong information about the effect of ketogenic diet. It is hard to switch diet just because the doctor recommended. Managing the amount of carbohydrates and medication at the same time can maintain blood sugar for diabetics.

Putting It All Together

I hope you have found this guide to a ketogenic diet helpful and informative. With the proper diet and exercise regimen, you can see incredible changes in your body in very little time.

For any diet to work, you need to take action and stay committed. It is easy to have a cheat day here and there, especially when you are missing your favorite foods, but don't give in to the temptation. One cheat day often leads to another, and you find yourself suddenly not making any progress. Stick with it and believe in yourself. You can do it!

Preview of "Essential Oils" by Emily V. Steinhauser

Essential Oils

Essential oils are oils that are extracted from the flowers, leaves, fruits, peel, seeds, woods, bark, roots, and other natural materials. There are thousands of different kinds of essential oils, and each has unique properties and characteristics. They are highly volatile so they are easily absorbed by the skin. So one wants to take care in the use of them.

Many body care products contain essential oils that they use for their therapeutic properties, and not just for their scent. There are many essential oils that are an effective treatment for a number of different skin conditions. They are extremely concentrated and powerful. They can be regenerative both in physical and emotional ways, making you feel healthy and stronger. The benefits cannot be understated, essential oils can have a dramatic impact on how you look and feel.

This book will explore the various ways that one can use essential oils. I will also present the best oils to use in each specific situation, both from research and personal experience. Sections will focus on the using essential oils to treat, heal, and rejuvenate one's skin. We will also explore how to use essential oils to thicken one's hair, promote faster hair re-growth, and how to deal with hair loss.

Essential oils are often used therapeutically, and I will talk about the medicinal uses of essential oils. I will not only focus on physical application of the oils, but also on aromatherapy and the benefits it provides.

One of my favorite uses of essential oils is using them to deal with headaches, including migraines. They also prove efficacious for first aid, particularly in the reduction of swelling and the healing of bruises. I will also present information on how you can use essential oils to sharpen your mental focus, improve your concentration, and enhance your overall memory.

I am excited that you have joined me on this journey through the essential oils. I hope they bring you a long lifetime of improved health and comfort.

I hope you enjoyed the free preview of "Essential Oils" by Emily V. Steinhauser.

Preview of "Kindle Publishing Secrets Revealed" by James Chen

Learn to Make Money with Kindle Books

Passive income. We all want to make it. And publishing books on Amazon Kindle is a great way to do it. Imagine your books earning money 24 hours a day, 365 days a year on autopilot, leaving you the time to do whatever you desire. Sounds like a wonderful life, right?

It can be, and the first step is publishing your book. This book will guide you step by step through the process, from initial research to how to market your book.

Don't think you are a very good writer? I will show you how outsource your ideas to other writers who will write the books for you. All you need to do is publish them. And collect the checks.

I will also divulge a secret niche which sees extraordinary sales and searches on Amazon. There are very few writers taking advantage of this trick, and those who have are seeing their books in the bestseller lists. The best part: this niche only requires the books be between 15 to 30 pages in length. Short books, huge rewards.

Learn to take advantage of Amazon's enormous customer base, publishing books that will be searched for, found, and purchased. Learn to get your books to stand out from the millions of other ones already available in the Kindle store. It is simple: if people cannot find your books, they will not buy them. Learn how to be found.

The #1 Rule of Kindle Marketing

The rule is simple: find a process that makes money. And repeat it. Over and over again. This rule is particularly effective in terms of Kindle publishing. You publish your book, market it, let it make money, and do the entire process again.

Too many writers concentrate on one book. They invest all of their energy in making it perfect, trying to build up and audience, instead of writing additional books. Understand that having one book found within millions of books requires a whole lot of luck. But if you have two books, your odds increase. Think of each book as a lottery ticket, the more you have, the more likely you will have one hit the jackpot. Your goal should not be to have one book in the Kindle store, but hundreds. Don't imagine yourself as a writer, but as a publisher. And act accordingly.

Authors often focus on the visible success stories on Amazon, on the fiction writers who have sold hundreds of thousands of books. This is an incredibly small group, and their success is hard to replicate, because it was brought about by luck. You will most likely never get this lucky, so you need to create your own success. That means publishing a lot of books.

The people making money in the system are those who publish hundreds of books under different pen names. These books are often outsourced to a group of writers, as are the formatting and cover creation. This book encourages you to embrace the second method and act like a publisher, producing and selling as much content as you can.

Remember the more you publish, the larger your slice of the pie will be.

I hope you enjoyed the free preview of "Kindle Publishing Secrets Revealed" by James Chen.

Other Books Available From Gamma Mouse Media

Below you will find other popular Amazon bestsellers from Gamma Mouse Media.

Essential Oils – Emily V. Steinhauser

Forex Indicators – Warren R. Sullivan

Kindle Publishing Secrets Revealed – James Chen

Procrastination – Warren R. Sullivan

Brain Training Boot Camp – Warren R. Sullivan

Knee Pain Treatment – Emily V. Steinhauser

Marriage Problems – Emily V. Steinhauser

Quiet – Amelia Austin

Lust for Me – Amelia Austin

Cellulite Reduction – Emily V. Steinhauser

The Quick Start Guide to Macarons – Lindsay Stotts

Speed Reading Training – Warren R. Sullivan

Memory Enhancement – Warren R. Sullivan

The Quick Start Guide to Perfect Pancakes – Lindsay Stotts

Compulsive Hoarding – Emily V. Steinhauser

Made in the USA
Middletown, DE
07 December 2015